© Copyright 2016

Written by Sally A Jones and Amanda C Jones
Illustrations by Annalisa Jones

Published by GUINEA PIG EDUCATION

2 Cobs Way,
New Haw,
Addlestone,
Surrey,
KT15 3AF.
www.guineapigeducation.co.uk

NO part of this publication may be reproduced, stored or copied for commercial purposes and profit without the prior written permission of the publishers.

ISBN: 9781910824030

Dear kids,

In this book, you will find some well-known stories. You will have heard them before, when you were younger. Read them again… and then try writing your own version. You can put some of your own ideas in.

Dear adults,

A collection of traditional tales for your child to read and then write their own version. Encourage them to use their imagination and to reinvent the story. For example, they could alter the plot and introduce a new ending.

Trialled by children of 6-9 years in our tutorial classes, we believe that if we saturate young children with good ideas and vocabulary, they will learn to love writing.

We recommend that you work through the book with younger children. Discuss the characters and where the story takes place; talk about how the story will begin; how it will continue; how it will build up to the most exciting part and how it will end. Older children will be able to work through the book themselves.

More for adults...

People have always made up stories. In early times, before people could read, short stories were told, retold and passed down the generations as folk tales.

Everyone can remember some of the traditional stories that they were told as small children, like 'Little Red Riding a Hood' or 'The Three Billy Goats Gruff'.

These stories often use rhyme or repetition to help us remember them. In 'The Three Little Pigs' the big, bad wolf 'huffs and puffs to blow the house down'. In the story; 'The Three Billy Goats Gruff', the goats 'trip, trap, trip trap over the iron bridge' using alliteration (words that begin with the same sound) or onomatopoeia (words that sound like the action) to create word pictures.

Find a notebook, a pen and a pencil.

Draw a cloud.

Draw or write what comes into your mind. Decide on a plot. Think about a title.

Think about the people or characters in your story.

Think about the place or setting. where the action happens in your story.

Let's make a plan.

The title is *'The Three Billy Goats Gruff.'*

1. Who are the characters in the story?

   Three billy goats and a troll

2. Where does the story take place?

   On a bridge and in a field of green grass.

3. What will happen?

   The three billy goats cross the bridge to get to the green grass on the other side, but they have to pass a big, bad troll.

Beginning

1. Introduce who is in the story

2. Where it happens

3. What they are going to do

Adults we call this <u>structuring</u> a story.

> First Paragraph
>
> *The little billy goat goes across the bridge. He persuades the troll not to eat him, because a bigger billy goat is coming.*

Middle

1. Now write what the characters do next

2. … and after this

3. Are you wondering what will happen?
   This is what we call suspense.

> Second Paragraph
>
> *The second billy goat goes across the bridge. He persuades the troll not to gobble him up, because an even bigger billy goat is coming.*

Ending

1. How does the story finish?

2. Is it a happy ending?

3. Is it sad?

4. Is there a lesson to be learnt?

5. Does it end suddenly (on a cliff hanger) so you have to make up your own ending?

End Paragraph

Big billy goat goes across the bridge. He meets the troll and tosses him into the water. The troll swims away.

Amber's Story

This story is told using the character's speech. We call it dialogue.

> Beginning
>
> Once upon a time, there were three little billy goats gruff. They wanted to get to the green grass on the other side of the bridge, but under the bridge there lived a big, bad troll.
>
> The first billy goat gruff set out to cross the bridge. 'Trip trap, trip, trap' he went, over the iron bridge.
> "Who's that crossing my bridge?" growled the big, bad troll.
> "It's only me, little billy goat gruff."
> "I'm coming to gobble you up," growled the big, bad troll.
> "Oh please don't gobble me up," pleaded the little billy goat gruff, "my brother is coming after me and he's bigger and juicier than me."
> "Very well," said the big, bad troll.

Middle

The second billy goat gruff, went 'trip trap, trip, trap' over the iron bridge.
"Who's that crossing my bridge?" growled the big, bad troll.
"It's only me," replied the second billy goat gruff."
"I'm coming to gobble you up," growled the big, bad troll.
"Oh please don't gobble me up," pleaded the second billy goat gruff, "my brother is coming after me and he's bigger and juicier than me."
"Very well," said the big, bad troll.

Ending

Now the third billy goat gruff, the biggest and strongest of the billy goats, went 'trip trap, trip, trap' over the iron bridge.
"Who's that crossing my bridge?" roared the big, bad troll.
"I'm coming to gobble you up,"
"Very well," replied the third billy goat gruff. The big, bad troll and the strongest billy goat met on the iron bridge. They faced each other. The big billy goat charged at the troll and tossed him over the bridge into the deep, dark water. The troll was so scared he swam away and was never seen again. Then, the big billy goat gruff went 'trip, trap, trip, trap' over the iron bridge to meet his brothers and together, they ate the delicious grass on the other side of the bridge.

Read this story again. Write 3 paragraphs of your own to tell the story. Write 3 - 5 sentences for each paragraph.

What happens next?

Try to imagine what happens after the troll left.

Here is a story that Deniz wrote.

Beginning

Once upon a time three big, hairy trolls arrived at an iron bridge. They had come to visit their friend Hulk, but he was not there. On the other side of the bridge, they saw some billy goats grazing on the green grass.

The three trolls approached the smallest billy goat,
"Tell me where we can find our friend Hulk?" they growled.
"He went that way," stammered little billy goat fearfully, pointing in the direction of the middle billy goat.

Middle

Then, the trolls approached the middle billy goat, who was tearing at the juicy grass with her sharp teeth,
"Tell me where we will find our friend Hulk," they each snarled in turn?
"He went that way," signalled the middle billy goat, pointing in the direction of the biggest billy goat gruff.

End

The largest billy goat was guarding the green grass, when he saw three mean looking trolls coming towards him. Big billy goat was not scared. He put his big horns down and prepared to fight. Before the trolls had time to question him, the biggest billy goat ran towards them and butted them with his sharp horns.

"If you are looking for your friend the troll, I can tell you, he went to the same place that you are going to," he grunted. The biggest billy goat chased the trolls down to the riverbank. All three trolls jumped in and swan away as fast as they could. No trolls were ever seen in the area again.

Talk about Deniz's story.

What would you write?

Write a 'what happens next' story.

Let's make a plan for the 'Three Little Pigs.'

Characters: A big bad wolf
Three little pigs

Setting: A town with houses.

The Plot: A big, bad wolf tries to catch three little pigs by blowing their houses down, but he cannot blow down the house of bricks.

First Paragraph

The little pig builds his house of straw. The big, bad wolf blows it down and the little pig runs away.

Once upon a time, there was a little pig who built a house of straw. There was a loud knock at the door. A gruff voice said, "Little pig, little pig, can I come in?"
"Oh no, not by the hairs on my chinny, chin, chin, I will not let you in," the little pig replied.
"Then I'll huff and I'll puff and I'll blow your house down." The big, bad wolf huffed and puffed and blew the house down.
"Help! Help!" shouted the little pig and he ran to his brother's house.

<u>Middle Paragraph</u>   What happens next?

The second little pig builds his house of sticks. The big, bad wolf blows it down and the little pig runs away.

The second little pig built a house of sticks. There was a loud knock at the door. A gruff voice said,
"Little pig, little pig, can I come in?"
"Oh no, not by the hairs on my chinny, chin, chin, I will not let you in," replied the pig.
"Then I'll huff and I'll puff and I'll blow your house down." The big, bad wolf huffed and puffed and blew the house down.
"Help! Help!" shouted the little pig and he ran to his brother's house.

End Paragraph

The third little pig builds his house of bricks. The big, bad wolf 'huffs and puffs' but he can't blow this house down. He enters the house by the chimney and falls into the hot cooking pot.

> The third little pig built a house of bricks.
> There was a loud knock at the door.
> A gruff voice said,
> "Little pig, little pig, please can I come in?"
> The pig replied,
> "Oh no, not by the hairs on my chinny, chin, chin, I will not let you in."
> "Then I'll huff and I'll puff and I'll blow your house down." The big, bad wolf huffed and puffed. He huffed and puffed again... and again, but he could not blow the house of bricks down.
> "Little pig, little pig, I'm coming down the chimney," he growled. The big, bad wolf climbed up onto the roof and down the chimney, but he fell straight into a big pot of hot stew cooking on the fire. The wolf ran out of the door and far away over the hill.

Read this story again. Cover it and write 3 paragraphs of your own.

What happens next?

Try to imagine what happens after the wolf fell down the chimney.

Here is a story that Selin wrote.

Beginning

Once upon a time the ground was covered in a white blanket of snow. Big, bad wolf was shivering. He had returned from hunting, but he couldn't find the entrance to his den. It was completely blocked by snow. He scrabbled at the snow, but he could not get in.

Middle

Big, bad wolf decided he would have to get some help... so he shuffled through the snow - slipping and sliding on his paws. Soon he came to a house of straw, but it had been blown down. Next, he came to a house of sticks, but this too had been blown down. Wolf felt sad because he had nowhere to go, but he trudged on up the hill, until he came to a smart house made of brick. He knocked on the door.
"I have lost my home. Please can I come in? Please help me," he cried.

End

Inside the house, the three little pigs looked at each other with alarm. "What shall we do?" they gasped. "We cannot leave our neighbour out in the cold even if he is a wolf." They opened the door and saw the big, bad wolf standing there, but there was something different about him. He had changed into a good wolf. He wasn't the big, bad wolf anymore. They invited him in for supper round the fire

Talk about Selin's story. What would you write? Now it's your turn to write one.

Let's make a plan for the story of '_Cinderella._'

Characters: A girl called Cinderella
Two ugly step sisters
A fairy godmother
A handsome prince

Setting: A kitchen in a cottage and a royal palace.

The Plot: A fairy godmother casts a magic spell, so that Cinderella can go to a ball at the palace. Here, she meets a prince, but at midnight she runs away because her clothes turn back to rags.

First Paragraph

Cinderella is made to work in the kitchen by her wicked stepsisters. A fairy godmother appears and uses her magic wand to turn Cinderella's ragged clothes into a beautiful dress. She turns a pumpkin into a coach and horses, so she can go to the ball at the palace.

<u>Middle Paragraph</u>   What happens next?

Cinderella goes to the ball and dances with a handsome prince. He falls in love with her. The clock strikes midnight but Cinderella has to run away from the palace, because her dress will turn back to rags and her carriage back to a pumpkin. In her hurry, she loses a shoe.

End Paragraph

The prince searches the whole country to find the girl who fits the shoe. He fits it on Cinderella's stepsisters but it does not fit either of them. He fits it on Cinderella and it does fit. The prince marries Cinderella and they live happily ever after.

Let's read Nina's version of the story.

> Once upon a time, there was a girl called Cinderella, who had two ugly stepsisters. They made her work in the kitchen. One day, the prince invited the family to a ball, but the ugly stepsisters wouldn't let Cinderella go.
>
> On the day of the ball, a fairy godmother appeared to Cinderella.
> She said,
> "You will go to the ball," and she waved her magic wand. She made a coach and horses out of a pumpkin for Cinderella to travel in. She made a beautiful dress for her to wear.
>
> Cinderella went to the ball. She was the most beautiful girl in the room. The handsome prince danced with her and he fell in love with her. The clock chimed midnight. Cinderella knew her beautiful dress would turn back to rags. She ran out of the palace.
>
> The next day, the prince found a shoe. It had been left behind by the beautiful girl he had danced with. The prince searched the kingdom to find the girl who fitted the shoe. He tried it on the two ugly sisters, but it didn't fit either of them. He tried it on Cinderella. It fitted. The prince married Cinderella and they lived happily ever after.

Cover this story and write it yourself.

What happens next?

Write a story about 'Cinderella's child.'

Here is one that Coralie wrote.

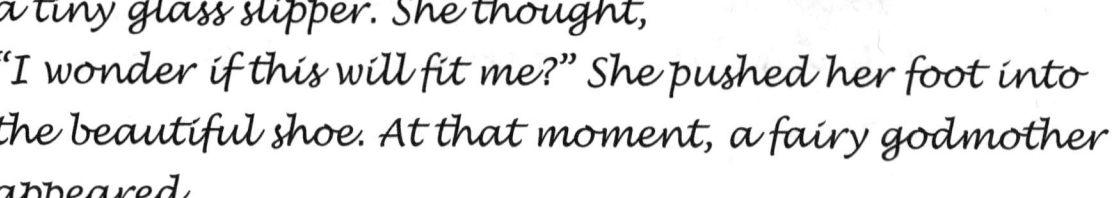

Cinderella and the prince lived happily together in their castle. After a little while, Queen Cinderella gave birth to the most beautiful child. The little girl had everything she wanted, but she grew up to be a sour, spoilt girl, who was never satisfied and always wanted more.

One day, when she was sixteen years old, she found a big, wooden chest. Inside, she found a tiny glass slipper. She thought, "I wonder if this will fit me?" She pushed her foot into the beautiful shoe. At that moment, a fairy godmother appeared.
"I will give you one wish," the fairy godmother grinned.
"I would like to see how ordinary girls live," replied the spoilt girl." Suddenly, she was in a small kitchen: scrubbing the floor, chopping vegetables and stirring a big pan. She looked down at her ragged clothes.
"Oh no," she cried. "What have I done?"

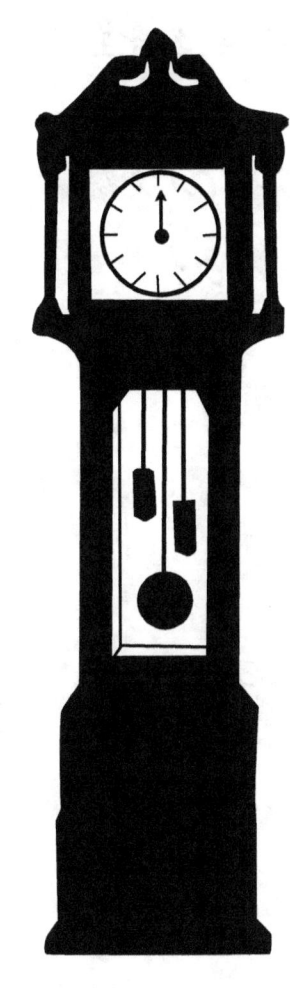

At that moment, the clock chimed midnight.

The princess found herself back in her palace, surrounded by beautiful things and holding her silk purse full of coins. There was no time to waste. The princess put on her coat and hat and headed out of the castle in the direction of the town.

"I must help the poor people," she thought. "I cannot keep all my money for myself. There are other people who need it more than me. From that time, wherever she could the princess helped the poor and she was never selfish again.

Let's make a plan for the story of '<u>Little Red Riding Hood.</u>'

> Characters: A girl dressed in red called Little Red Riding Hood.
> Her grandmother.
> A wolf.
> A woodcutter.
>
> Setting: A little cottage in the wood.
>
> The Plot: An evil wolf pretends to be Little Red Riding Hood's grandmother and hides in her bed. She is rescued by a woodcutter.

Paragraph one: A little girl sets out to visit her sick grandmother, but meets a wolf in the wood.

Paragraph two: The girl is talking to her grandmother in her bed but she looks different.

Paragraph three: The wolf chases Little Red Riding Hood, but a woodcutter rescues her.

Let's read Jay's version of the story.

One day a girl called Little Red Riding Hood went to visit her sick grandmother, to take her a basket of food. She lived in a cottage deep in the wood. On the way, she met an evil wolf and he asked her where she was going. She told the wolf that she was going to her grandmother's house. The wolf licked his lips and he ran off.

Little Red Riding Hood knocked at the door of her grandmother's cottage.
A gruff voice answered,
"Come in". She entered the room and saw granny tucked up in bed.
"What big ears you have grandmother," she whispered.
"All the better to hear you with my dear," replied the grandmother.
"What a long, pointed nose you have."
"All the better to smell you with my dear," replied the grandmother.
"What big, sharp teeth you have grandmother,"
"All the better to eat you up with…" and with this, the wolf jumped out of grandmother's bed and chased Little Red Riding Hood round the room.

A woodcutter heard Little Red Riding Hood screaming and he ran to help her. When he saw the wolf, he tried to catch him, but the wolf ran away out of the door. Little Red Riding Hood and the woodcutter rescued grandmother from her hiding place in the wardrobe. She was so pleased to see them that she was soon well again.

Cover this story and see if you can write your own version.

Now try writing this well-known tale as one of the characters in the story.

Write Grandmother's story.

> Once upon a time, there was a kindly old grandma, who lived in a pretty little thatched cottage deep in the woods. She had fallen and hurt her knee and so she had to rest. Everyday, after school, her little grand daughter Red Riding Hood, brought her a basket of food that her mum had cooked.
>
> One day, grandma was lying in her bed when there was a ring at the doorbell. She jumped out of bed and hobbled over to the door. "Come in dear," she uttered jovially. "How kind of you...," came a deep voice. To grandma's horror in strolled an enormous grey wolf, which grinned at her through an open mouth of razor sharp teeth. Grandma screamed loudly. The wolf tried to grab grandma, but she ran up the stairs and hid in the wardrobe terrified.

After a while, there was some shouting downstairs. Then, a woodcutter appeared and called up to Grandma.

"I've chased the wolf away. It's safe to come down." He helped her out of the wardrobe. Grandma was pleased to see them. Grandma and Little Red Riding Hood went on the internet. They bought some strong locks for the windows and doors, so grandma would have peace of mind that she was safe.

Let's plan the story of '*Jack and the Beanstalk.*'

Characters: A lazy boy, called Jack.
Jack's mum
An old woman
A fearsome giant

Setting: A road on the way to market.
A giants castle at the top of the beanstalk.

The Plot: A poor boy sells a cow in exchange for some magic beans. The beans grow into a beanstalk. Jack climbs to the top of it and steals gold from the giant.

First paragraph:

Jack sells a cow for some beans, but his angry mother throws them out of the window.

Middle paragraph: What happens next?

The beans grow into an enormous beanstalk. Jack climbs to the top of it, where he finds a giant. Jack steals the giant's gold.

End paragraph:

The giant chases Jack, but the boy climbs down the beanstalk to the ground quickly and chops it down with an axe.

Let's read Nina's version of the story.

Once there was a foolish boy, who lived with his mother. The family were very poor, so the boy sold his cow in exchange for some magic beans. His mother was so angry that she threw the beans out of the window.

Next morning, Jack saw an enormous beanstalk had grown from the beans. Jack climbed up it. At the top of the beanstalk, there was a castle. It belonged to a fierce giant who had a pot of gold. The giant was asleep, so Jack crept up to him and stole his gold. At that moment, the giant opened his eyes. He saw Jack with his gold and he was very angry. He shouted, "Fee Fi Fo Fum, I smell the blood of an Englishman."

The giant chased Jack down the beanstalk, but the boy was very fast. He reached the bottom before the giant. Jack grabbed an axe and cut the beanstalk down: that was the end of the big, bad giant. Jack and his mother became rich and lived happily ever after.

What happens next?

Can you carry on the story? Here are some ideas you can use.

PLAN

> 1) One night the giant's friend knocks at the door and asks for the gold back
>
> 2) The giant's friend kidnaps Jack in the middle of the night and takes him back to the castle in the clouds
>
> 3) He sends a ransom note to Jack's mother. She must return the gold and Jack will be returned unharmed.
>
> 4) The police are called and Jack is arrested for stealing the giant's possessions.

Let's plan the story of '<u>Sleeping Beauty</u>.'

Characters: A beautiful young princess, called Sleeping Beauty.
A good fairy.
A wicked witch.
A handsome prince.

Setting: A castle in a magical land.

The Plot: A wicked witch puts a spell upon a princess. On her sixteenth birthday, she will prick her finger and fall asleep. The spell may only be broken by the kiss from a handsome prince.

First Paragraph

A beautiful princess is born. Some good fairies bring gifts to the baby, but a wicked witch casts a spell saying she will prick her finger and fall into a deep sleep.

Middle Paragraph What happens next?

On her sixteenth birthday, Sleeping Beauty enters a room with a spinning wheel. She pricks her finger and falls into a deep sleep. For one hundred years the whole castle sleeps with her.

End Paragraph

A gallant prince rides by and cuts down the thorny bushes, which have grown around the castle. He kisses the princess and she wakes up. He falls in love with her.

Let's read Serena's version of the story.

> Once upon a time a beautiful baby girl was born in a castle. Her parents were very happy. Some good fairies came to give the baby gifts, but a wicked witch appeared and cast a spell. She announced that the girl would prick her finger on a spinning wheel and die. Everyone was sad, so a good fairy cast another spell and said she would only fall asleep and wake after a hundred years.
>
> On the princesses sixteenth birthday, she was exploring the castle when she saw a room that she had never been in before and opened the door. Inside, she saw an old lady spinning at a spinning wheel. The old woman showed her how to spin, but she pricked her finger. The terrible spell started to work and Sleeping Beauty fell into a deep, deep sleep. Everyone in the whole kingdom fell asleep.
>
> One hundred years later, a gallant prince rode by on his horse. He cut down the thorny bushes that had grown up around the castle with his sword. He entered the castle and saw the princess asleep on a bed. He kissed her and she woke up. Then, the whole kingdom woke up. The prince married Sleeping Beauty and they lived happily ever after.

Now cover. Can you re-tell the story?

What happens next?

Can you carry on the story? Here are some ideas.

PLAN

> 1) Sleeping Beauty has woken up after a hundred years, but her old enemy, the wicked witch, is still making her life difficult.
>
> 2) Sleeping Beauty orders some modern clothes, but the wicked witch makes sure they don't arrive.
>
> 3) Sleeping Beauty buys herself a computer, but the wicked witch hacks into it.
>
> 4) Sleeping Beauty buys some modern machines, but the wicked witch casts a spell on them and they break down.

Think of your own ideas and write a story.

This poem tells the story:

There was a princess long-ago,
Long-ago, long-ago.
There was a princess long-ago,
Long, long-a-go.

And she lived in a big high tower,
A big high tower, a big high tower,
And she lived in a big high tower,
Long, long-a-go.

One day a fairy waved her wand,
Waved her wand, waved her wand.
One day a fairy waved her wand,
Long, long a-go.

The princess slept for a hundred years,
A hundred years, a hundred years.
The princess slept for a hundred years,
Long, long a-go.

A great big forest grew around,
Grew around, grew around.
A great big forest grew around,
Long, long a-go.

A handsome Prince came riding by,
Riding by, riding by.
A handsome Prince came riding by,
Long, long a-go.

He took his sword and cut it down,
Cut it down, cut it down.
He took his sword and cut it down,
Long, long a-go.

He kissed her hand to wake her up,
Wake her up, wake her up.
He kissed her hand to wake her up,
Long, long ago.

So everybody's happy now,
Happy now, happy now -
so everybody's happy now,
Ha-ppy now.

Here are some more well known stories. Get an adult to help you copy or cut out the pages. Cut along the dotted lines and muddle them up. Now, sort them back into the right order. Read the story. Cover it and re-write your own version, putting in more detail.

Think of some more traditional tales that are not in this book. Read them and try writing your own version.

Can you see that all the stories have a beginning, a middle and an end?

Rapunzel
Snow White

ROBIN HOOD

There was once an outlaw called Robin Hood.

He lived in Sherwood Forest with his band of merry men.

One day Robin, and his men, attacked Nottingham Castle with their bows and arrows.

They broke into the castle and stole money from the rich sheriff.

The Sheriff of Nottingham sent soldiers to catch Robin Hood,

but they could not find him because he was hiding in the forest.

Robin Hood gave the money he had stolen to the poor.

GOLDILOCKS AND THE THREE BEARS

Once upon a time there was a girl called Goldilocks, who went for a walk in the woods.

She saw a pretty cottage.

The door was open, so she went in.

At the table, there were three chairs. She tried each one. She liked the smallest chair best, but it broke when she sat on it

On the table, there were three bowls of porridge. She tasted them all, but she liked the smallest bowl of porridge best and ate it all up.

In the next room, there were three beds. She lay down on each one, but she fell asleep in the smallest bed, because it was the most cosy.

The three bears came home to the cottage.

Daddy bear growled loudly,

"Who has been sitting on my big chair?"

Mummy bear grunted gently, "Who has been sitting on my middle sized chair?"

Baby bear spoke softly,
 "Who has been sitting on my tiny chair and has broken it to bits?"

Daddy bear growled furiously,
 "Who has been eating my big bowl of porridge?" Mummy bear grunted gently,
 "Who has been eating my middle sized bowl of porridge?"
Baby bear spoke softly,
 "Who has been eating my tiny bowl of porridge and has gobbled it right up?"

Then they went to the bedroom.
Daddy bear growled loudly,
 "Who has been sleeping in my big bed?"
Mummy bear grunted gently,
 "Who has been sleeping in my middle sized bed?"
Baby bear spoke softly,
 "Who has been sleeping in my tiny bed and is still there?"

At that moment Goldilocks woke up. She saw the bears and ran out of the house. She never came back.

THE GINGERBREAD MAN

One day an old woman baked a gingerbread man.

She mixed the batter, rolled out the dough and put him in the oven to cook.

When she opened the oven door, he jumped out, saying,
"Run, run as fast as you can. You can't catch me, I'm a gingerbread man."

While he was running, the gingerbread man met a cow that wanted to eat him, but the gingerbread man shouted,
"I ran from the old woman and I can run away from you. Run, run as fast as you can. You can't catch me, I'm a gingerbread man."

Next, he met a horse, that wanted to eat him, but the gingerbread man shouted,
"I ran from the old woman and the cow and I can run away from you. Run, run as fast as you can. You can't catch me, I'm a gingerbread man."

He met a chicken, that wanted to peck him, but the gingerbread man shouted, "I'm racing from an old woman, a cow and a horse and I can run away from you. Run, run as fast as you can. You can't catch me, I'm a gingerbread man."

Then he met a fox. The fox saw the gingerbread man running away. He was being chased by an old woman, a cow, a horse and a chicken.

The fox whispered reassuringly, "Hop on my back and I'll take you across the river to safety."

The gingerbread man hopped onto his back and the fox started to swim across the river.

Then SNAP, the fox took a bite, a second and a third. The gingerbread man was all gone.

HANSEL AND GRETAL
A modern version

There was once a brother and sister. They were called Hansel and Gretel.

Their wicked stepmother took them into the woods and left them there, because the family had no money.

In the woods Hansel and Gretel came across a little house.

Its roof was made of chocolate, its walls were made of cake and the windows and doors were made of sweets.

The children were hungry, so they broke pieces off and ate them. Delicious!

A wicked witch, who lived in the house, saw the children eating.

The witch grabbed them and pushed them into a cage.

Then, the witch heated the oven to prepare dinner.

The children were scared, but Gretel was clever. She picked the lock of the cage and the children escaped and ran out of the door.

They ran back to their father and reported the witch to the police. She was arrested and put in prison. The children took the gold in the house to their father. They lived happily ever after.

THE MERMAID

There was once a beautiful mermaid.

Her body was half human and half fish.

One day, she took off her fish skin and lay it on the rocks to comb her long, copper coloured hair.

A young man walked by the ocean.

He saw a strange fish skin lying on the rocks. He took it home and locked it in a box, but he lost the key.

Later, a beautiful girl came to his door looking for her fish skin. The man fell in love with her and asked her to be his wife.

The couple had three children.

One day the boy child found a key, it fitted the box and he found the fish skin.

He showed his mother the fish skin.

She remembered her life as a mermaid.

She did not want to leave her children, but the call of the sea was too strong.

She went back to the sea,

but at night she came back and left her children gifts.

THREE WISHES

Once upon a time there was a poor woodcutter.

He went to the forest to cut down an oak tree with his axe.

As he started to chop it down, he heard a little cry.

A fairy appeared.

She begged him to spare the tree.

Because he was a kind man, he did not cut down the tree.

The fairy was grateful so she granted him three wishes.

When he arrived home he was hungry, but there was nothing in the cupboards,

so he wished for a black pudding.

At that moment, a black pudding clattered down the chimney.

His wife asked him where the pudding came from, but she did not believe his story about the fairy. She wished the pudding would stick to his face.

As if by magic, the pudding stuck to his face.

Then, they wished the pudding would come off.

Soon it lay back on a dish and they ate it for tea,

but they had wasted all their wishes.

What can you remember about stories?

Stories have settings.

Stories have characters.

Stories have a plot.

Stories have action.

Stories have a beginning, a middle and an end.

Stories have suspense (the bit that makes the reader want to read on).

Stories are fun and entertain us

Stories have happy endings, sad endings, cliff hanger endings and sometimes a moral ending

There are different sorts of stories

When we read a fairy tale we use our imagination

Make up your own story. It might be a 'once upon a time story' or an imaginative story

> 1. Your child must think of a title.
> 2. He or she can also decide on characters.
> 3. Who will be in the story?
> 4. What do they look like and behave like?

Characters might be:
- a magic fairy
- a princess
- three pigs
- a prince

He or she can decide on the <u>setting</u>.

Where will the story take place?

The setting might start in a castle and then go into the wild wood.

> What is the plot?
>
> He or she can decide on the <u>plot</u>?
>
> A wicked witch might turn a prince into a pig, but a princess breaks the spell with her magic wand.

How does the story begin?

A princess has her sixteenth birthday, but she needs a prince to marry.

How does the story continue? What happens after that? ... and after that? ...and after that?

A fairy appears and tells the princess that a prince has been turned into a pig by a spell.

How does the story end?

She touches him on the nose and he turns back to a prince.

The Pig Prince

Long ago in a faraway land, a beautiful girl called Rosa was out walking on her own. A fairy appeared in front of her and pleaded with her to help. She told her that a wicked witch had cast a spell and had turned a handsome, young prince into a pig.
"The spell," she continued, "can only be broken if a beautiful, young girl touches the pig's nose with a magic wand. At this, she handed the girl a wand and disappeared.

What could she do? Princess Rosa set off for the secret forest immediately. Before long, she met a pig and touched it on the nose with the wand.

"The spell is broken," she cried, but it only squealed loudly and ran off. It was not long before the girl met a second pig. She ran up to him and tapped him on the nose with the wand.

"The spell is broken," she cried even louder, but the pig grunted loudly and raced off.

"Where will I find this poor prince?" she wailed sadly.

At that very moment, she met a third pig. He was a fine looking animal and he turned and looked at her with his bright, blue eyes.

Immediately the princess touched him on the nose.

"The spell is broken," she screamed. There was a big bang and a puff of smoke and the pig turned back into a boy. The boy and girl fell in love with each other. They got married and lived happily ever after.

Make up your own princess story.

A modern fairy tale set in Romania by Alex

Snow had fallen heavily all night long. It lay deep and crisp on the hills and ice cream trees glistened in the winter sunshine. Two brothers, Stefan and Albert, who lived in a nearby cottage, were slipping and sliding in the snow; they were tumbling off their sledges as they sped down the slopes and they were hurling snowballs at each other. They were having great fun in the newly fallen snow, but suddenly they sensed something watching them.

They noticed a shadow. There was something lurking in the deep snow. Then, they heard a howl... Both boys turned round instantly and froze with fright. The grey eyes of a wolf stared straight at them. He was not alone. Behind him was a whole pack of wolves.

"Hurl a snowball at them," cried Albert, eying the leader of the pack.

"Quick, throw it now," he shrieked.

"It is only making them more angry," gasped Stephan. "They are advancing on us and there's no way out. Eek!"

At that moment, a shot was fired. It went 'BANG' up into the air. It was followed by another one. The wolves looked agitated; they looked nervous. They tossed their heads and looked around. Then, they ran fast. They ran away back into the dark forest.

"Thank you," shouted both boys to the hunter. "They've come down from the mountains to find food in the villages," he shouted. "They won't bother you again." Then, the boys raced back home to tell their parents of their escape.

PARENTS READ WITH YOUR CHILD WHEN YOUR CHILD IS YOUNG

Retell a traditional story. Make it your own story.

Talk:
- about the characters
- the places (or setting)
- the plot
- add a different beginning or ending
- include a message

Add your own ideas.

1. Think about the different characters view points

2. Tell the story as if you were the giant in Jack and the Beanstalk...

3. ... because different characters will see the story differently.

Remember when you use:

- 'I' (or first person) the story is told from the story teller's point of view.

- 'he' or 'she' (third person) it means someone else tells the story, like a fly on the wall watching.

Tell traditional stories to your young children.

Tell legends, myths and fables.

You can make them interesting by altering the tone of your voice, by using gestures, actions and even puppets.

Don't just alter the tone of your voice, alter the pitch of your voice, the pace at which you read and your facial expressions to bring stories alive (and to create atmosphere).

If you add rhymes it will make stories memorable.

Remember the story of Snow White…

"Mirror, mirror on the wall, who is the fairest of them all…"

Repeat words and phrases and emphasise punctuation.

www.ingramcontent.com/pod-product-compliance
Lightning Source LLC
Chambersburg PA
CBHW050715090526
44587CB00019B/3391

GREYSCALE

BIN TRAVELER FORM

Cut By _Jesandrew Begley_ R 12 Qty _55_ Date _5-21_

Scanned By _____ Qty _____ Date _____

Scanned Batch IDs

Notes / Exceptions